CAN
SCIENCE
SOLVE ?

THE MYSTERY OF THE
LOCH NESS MONSTER

Holly Wallace

Heinemann Library
Chicago, Illinois

Customer Service 888-454-2279
Visit our website at www.heinemannraintree.com

Designed by Victoria Bevan and Q2A
Printed and bound in China by WKT

10 09 08 07 06
10 9 8 7 6 5 4 3 2 1

New edition ISBNs: 1-40348-337-X (hardcover)
                   1-40348-346-9 (paperback)

The Library of Congress has cataloged the hardcover editions as follows:
Wallace, Holly, 1961-
        The mystery of the Loch Ness Monster / Holly Wallace.
        p. cm. - (Can science solve?)
Includes bibliographical references (p.) and index.
Summary: Examines the history of the Loch Ness monster story, eyewitness accounts, various efforts to discover and identify the creature, explanations for its identity, and attempts to fake its appearances.
        ISBN 1-57572-805-2 (lib. bdg.)
        1. Loch Ness monster—Juvenile literature. [1. Loch Ness
monster. 2. Monsters.] I. Title. II. Series
QL89.2.L6W25   1999
001.944— dc21

                                        98-54481
                                            CIP
                                             AC

Acknowledgments
The author and publishers are grateful to the following for permission to reproduce copyright material:
Express Newspaper: p. 11; Fortean Picture Library: p. 7, L Coleman p. 18, R Dahinden p. 26, H Gray p10, A Hepburn p. 22, I Newby pp. 5, 16, ProjectUrquhart p. 28, A Shiels p. 4, D Stacy p. 12, R Wilson p. 24, N Witchell p. 15; Gamma: p. 27; Oxford Scientific Films: N Benvie p. 13, T Crabtree p. 21, L Rhodes p. 19.

Cover picture of the Loch Ness Monster, reproduced with permission of Science Photo Library/Victor Habbick Visions.

Every effort has been made to contact copyright holders of any material reproduced in this book. Any omissions will be rectified in subsequent printings if notice is given to the publisher.

The paper used to print this book comes from sustainable sources.

Some words are shown in bold, **like this**. You can find the definitions for these words in the glossary.

CONTENTS

UNSOLVED MYSTERIES

For hundreds of years, people have been interested in and puzzled by mysterious places, creatures, and events. Did the lost land of Atlantis ever exist? Are UFOs tricks of the light or actually vehicles from outer space? Who is responsible for mysterious crop circle patterns—clever fakers or alien beings? Is there really a monster living in Loch Ness? Some of these mysteries have baffled scientists, who have spent years trying to find the answers. But just how far can science go? Can it really explain the seemingly unexplainable? Are there some mysteries that science simply cannot solve? Read on, and make up your own mind . . .

This book tells you about the history of the Loch Ness Monster, using eyewitness accounts and photographic and scientific evidence. It looks at famous fakes and the different theories about whether the monster actually exists and what type of creature it is.

This is the most famous image of the Loch Ness Monster as a large, long-necked creature with a small head. This photograph, taken in 1977, seemed to show the monster, but computer analysis later proved it to be a fake.

What is the Loch Ness Monster?

There have been thousands of rumors and reports of mysterious monsters lurking in the world's deepest lakes. The most famous of all is the Loch Ness Monster. The word *loch* is Scottish for "lake." Loch Ness, in the Scottish Highlands, is Great Britain's largest lake. At 950 feet (290 meters) deep at its greatest depth, it is so deep that it could swallow up some of the world's tallest buildings. It is more than 300 million years old—a huge, gaping crack in Earth's surface, opened up by ancient rock movements. Today, monster-hunters can drive around the lake on modern roads, but this was not always so. Until the 18th century, the lake was practically impossible to reach, except by remote, winding trails. For millions of years, a monster could have been living in the lake, hidden away from prying eyes.

Modern reports of the Loch Ness Monster began in the 1930s, when a new road made the lake easier to reach and newly developed cameras enabled ordinary people to take photographs. Many of these photos have since been proved to be fakes. So, is there a monster in Loch Ness? We have thousands of supposed eyewitness accounts, some more believable than others. However, no traces of an actual monster have ever been found. Is there anything science can do to solve the mystery?

The cloudy depths of Loch Ness can now be explored by water and air. But what, if anything, do they hide?

THE MYSTERY BEGINS

Modern sightings of the Loch Ness Monster began in the 1930s, when a new road made the lake easier to reach . . . and to watch. However, the first accounts of the monster appeared long before this.

The saint and the monster

The first written report of a monster appeared in about C.E. 565, in the biography of an Irish saint, St. Columba, written about a century after his death by another monk, St. Adamnan. In it he tells how, one day, St. Columba arrived at the lakeshore to board the ferry. But the ferry was nowhere to be seen, so one of St. Columba's disciples volunteered to swim across and fetch a boat from the other side. As he dived in, a hideous monster suddenly rose to the surface and swam toward him. Everyone who saw it was "stricken with very great terror." But St. Columba prevented disaster by making the sign of the cross and ordering the monster to go away. At his words, it is said to have turned and disappeared.

Searching for evidence

Most scientists are doubtful about the existence of a Loch Ness Monster. Without hard scientific evidence, nothing can be proved. But the nature of the lake makes finding proof extremely difficult. The first problem is its sheer size. Loch Ness is enormous—22 miles (36 kilometers) long by about 1 mile (1.6 kilometers) wide, and with a maximum depth of 787 feet (240 meters). Second, its water is very brown and cloudy, severely reducing visibility under water. Yet people keep on looking . . .

Water horses

Scottish folklore is full of stories of mischievous spirits, called kelpies, that live in lakes. These are mentioned in several old books about Loch Ness. They are said to lurk by the lakeside, disguised as horses, waiting for human victims to eat. Local children were often warned not to swim in the lake for fear of the kelpies. Could the origins of the Loch Ness Monster lie with them?

Kelpies were Scottish spirits said to live in and around lakes. Rumors said that they attacked and ate people. The monster mystery may well have begun with them.

EYEWITNESS ACCOUNTS

Since the very first accounts, there have been 10,000 known eyewitness sightings of the monster, although only one-third have been recorded. The early 1930s, after the completion of the new road along the north shore of the lake, were a time of many sightings. Here are some of the most famous of them.

Mr. and Mrs. John Mackay

On April 14, 1933, the Mackays were returning home to Drumnadrochit, Scotland. It was about 3 o'clock in the afternoon. Suddenly, Mrs. Mackay noticed a disturbance on the lake. As her husband pulled up, a large animal surged up from the water and swam to the far shore. The Mackays glimpsed two black humps, rising and falling in the water, and then the creature sank from sight. News of their sighting reached the ears of a local journalist, and the Loch Ness Monster **phenomenon** was born.

Brother Richard Horan

Brother Richard Horan was a monk from St. Benedict's Abbey (monastery) on the shore of the lake at Fort Augustus, Scotland. On May 26, 1934, he was working in the abbey boathouse when he heard a noise in the water. He turned and saw that he was being watched by a large creature with a long, graceful neck, a white stripe down its front, and a muzzle (snout) like a seal's. Other monks also reported seeing the monster.

Mr. and Mrs. George Spicer

Three months later, the Spicers were driving back to London, England, after a vacation in Scotland. It was about 4 o'clock in the afternoon. About 650 feet (200 meters) ahead of them, they saw a long, dark shape stretched across the road. As they drew closer, they realized that it was a long, gray neck, followed by a gray body about 5 feet (1.5 meters) high. Mr. Spicer described it as looking like "a huge snail with a long neck." It shot across the road with a jerky movement before disappearing into bushes. "It was horrible," Spicer added. After this sighting, interest in Loch Ness grew worldwide. Huge prizes were offered for the monster, dead or alive.

The Spicers drew a picture of the monster they had seen. It looked like no other animal.

Mass hallucinations?

Despite the wealth of eyewitness accounts, scientists are still suspicious. After all, they argue, people's memories often play tricks on them, and perhaps wishful thinking has a large part to play. One scientist dismissed the sightings as "a striking example of mass **hallucination**." But could they all be wrong?

CAUGHT ON FILM

Some eyewitnesses have been able to capture the monster on film. Their photographs and films are greeted with great excitement. However, controversy often follows, since many have turned out to be fakes. You can read more about fake photos on pages 24 and 25.

First photograph

The first photograph of "Nessie," as the monster became known, was taken on November 12, 1933, by a walker named Hugh Gray. He snapped the monster as it rose out of the water about 650 feet (200 meters) in front of him. The photo was not very clear, but seemed to show the vague, grayish body of a large creature. The photograph appeared in two newspapers: the *Scottish Daily Record* and the *London Daily Sketch*. An expert **zoologist** from Glasgow University, in Scotland, dismissed it scornfully as not being like any living creature he had ever seen.

When Hugh Gray's photograph of the Loch Ness Monster was first published in 1933, it caused a huge stir. The monster quickly became known across the world.

Three humps

Early on July 14, 1951, local forestry worker Lachlan Stuart was milking his cows when he spotted something racing down the lake. At first he thought it must be a speedboat. Then, he noticed three large humps on its back. He rushed inside to fetch his camera and snapped the monster just 165 feet (50 meters) offshore. However, he was only able to take one photo before his camera jammed. Many people thought that Stuart's photo was genuine, though later research showed that it probably showed a group of rocks in shallow water near the shore.

Lachlan Stuart's photograph clearly shows three rounded shapes, possibly the humps of a huge monster. Doubters claimed that they were rocks.

Moving pictures

The first moving pictures of Nessie were taken in April 1960 by engineer Tim Dinsdale. Using a 16mm movie camera, he took several feet of film showing a hump swimming away from him. When shown on television, it caused a huge stir. But did it really show a monster? Six years later, the film was analyzed by British Royal Air Force Intelligence, which reported that the object was not a boat or submarine, but "probably **animate**." It was about 5.5 feet (1.7 meters) wide and was moving at about 10 miles (16 kilometers) per hour. It was also examined by computer-enhancement experts at **NASA**, who spotted two other parts that could belong to a body, apart from the main hump. Many people were convinced that this was the monster.

IT'S OFFICIAL!

Interest in Loch Ness continued to grow in the 1960s and 1970s with a new generation of monster-hunters. Despite the doubts of many scientists, serious **expeditions** were organized by colleges and local biologists to search the lake in search of proof that the monster existed, or equally, that it did not.

A full-time job

In 1969 Londoner Frank Searle gave up his job to camp full-time by Loch Ness. In 1971 his patience was rewarded. He described the monster as being "seven feet long, dark and knobbly on top, smooth dirty white underneath." More sightings followed, as did a series of photographs. Sadly, the films later proved to have been tampered with. In some, an extra hump had been **superimposed** onto the original photo!

Since the 1930s, thousands of people have visited Loch Ness in the hope of glimpsing the monster. Their starting point is often the Loch Ness Visitor Center on the shore of the lake.

Monster bureau

In 1961 the Loch Ness Investigation Bureau was founded by British **naturalist** Sir Peter Scott to explore the lake more systematically. The bureau collected all the existing sightings and organized a long-term watch over the lake. Night after night, teams of scientists scoured the lake with searchlights and **sonar.** They detected several large objects in the water, but could not identify what they were.

The Loch Ness Project

The Loch Ness Project was founded in 1978. It organizes field trips for students who volunteer to work on the lake. One of their tasks is to take samples of the **sediment** on the bottom of the lake. These are used for finding out more about the history of the lake, which may help to determine what type of creature the monster could be. The leader of the project is naturalist Adrian Shine. After twenty years of searching, he is now convinced that there is no Loch Ness Monster to be found.

Playing tricks

One of the problems with eyewitness evidence is that the lake itself plays tricks on the eyes. On a calm day, the steep shorelines cause deceptive shadows and reflections. These can make objects such as water birds, otters, boat **wakes,** and waves appear much bigger or longer than they actually are. Logs, mats of floating vegetation, and even speedboats have also been mistaken for monsters. So, is the monster an **optical illusion** or a case of mistaken identity, as many scientists suspect?

This is a European otter.

13

SEARCHING UNDERWATER

For people determined to find a monster in Loch Ness, the best place to look is, of course, under the water. If a monster does exist, this is where it must spend most of its time. Sending human divers down into the lake is a risky business. The water is very cold, very deep, and very cloudy. Scientists have had to find other ways to explore the lake. The two most effective methods used so far are sonar searching and underwater photography.

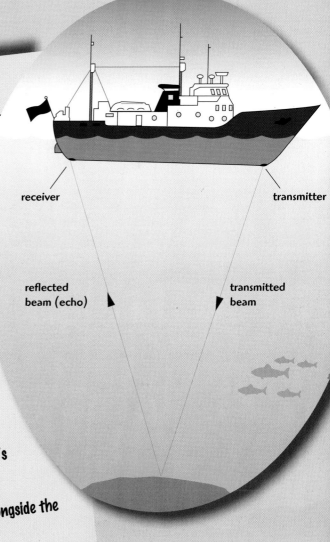

receiver

transmitter

reflected beam (echo)

transmitted beam

How sonar works

• The word sonar stands for "sound navigation and ranging."

• A sonar machine on board a boat sends out a pulse of sound in a narrow beam and listens for echoes as the sound bounces off objects in the water.

• From the time it takes for any echo to return, the machine figures out how far away the objects are.

• The direction and distance of the objects appear on a screen.

• Sonar can also give an idea of an object's size, shape, and speed.

• Some sonar machines can be towed alongside the boat to give a wider coverage.

Sonar searching

The first scientific **expedition** to Loch Ness was organized in 1959 by the Natural History Museum in London. Using sonar, scientists detected a large object just under the water's surface. They tracked it as it dived to a depth of 65 feet (20 meters) and then rose back up again. The object may have been a **shoal** of fish. A more recent expedition was Operation Deepscan in 1987. A **flotilla** of 24 boats, equipped with sonar, spent a week patrolling the lake. They detected a mysterious object that they described as being "the size of a large shark."

This shows a row of sonar boats scanning Loch Ness in search of a monster, during Operation Deepscan in 1987. Various mysterious, and still unidentified, objects were detected in the water.

Mistaken identity?

Hundreds of sonar "hits" have been made. You can even hire your own monster-hunting boat from the lakeshore, complete with sonar equipment. These hits seem to show that there are large animals living in Loch Ness. But, scientifically, they still do not represent concrete proof. Most of them could easily have been made by large shoals of fish, rising bubbles of gas in the water, or even giant underwater waves. Some, however, including three detected by Operation Deepscan, are yet to be identified . . .

UNDERWATER PHOTOGRAPHY

In 1972 and 1975 a team of scientists from the Academy of Applied Science, based in Massachusetts and led by Dr. Robert Rines, made a series of trips to Loch Ness. Working with the Loch Ness Investigation Bureau, they set up automatic cameras under the water to flash every few seconds or so, or whenever their sonar detected objects moving nearby. To their great excitement, several of the photographs appeared to show parts of a large creature.

Robert Rines fixed an underwater camera to a frame during his return to Loch Ness in 1980. Taking photographs underwater was made more difficult by the lake's cloudy water.

The flipper picture

One of the 1972 photographs seemed to show a large, diamond-shaped flipper. The 1975 photos showed the head and body of a large creature, which led **naturalist** Sir Peter Scott to suggest that the monster might have been a **plesiosaur,** a **prehistoric** reptile thought to be long **extinct** (see pages 18 and 19). The photographs were sent to other leading **zoologists** and even debated in the British Parliament, the main governmental body in Great Britain. One scientist went as far as to say that the photos seemed to indicate the presence of large animals in the lake, but were not enough to identify them. Others were not so sure.

Could this be the Loch Ness Monster? Rines's famous photograph, taken in 1972, seemed to show a flipper belonging to a large, swimming creature.

Return to Loch Ness

In 1997 Robert Rines returned to Loch Ness to try to prove once and for all that something was lurking in its water. With him, he brought Charles Wyckoff, a photographic pioneer who had developed the techniques needed to photograph nuclear bomb explosions and the surface of the Moon. The aim was to sweep the lake with sonar, then relay the results to a **GPS** (Global Positioning System) on the shore to give any object's exact location. The camera crew would follow closely behind. Although the sonar detected several large, moving targets that the team's **marine biologist** could not explain as **shoals** of fish, taking clear photographs proved a much trickier task. The cloudy water limited visibility to a few feet or so, and moisture seeped in and ruined the cameras. So, the mystery remains to be solved.

WHAT IS IT?

What type of monster do eyewitnesses claim to have seen? Their reports are remarkably similar, often describing a large, long-necked, hump-backed creature. It sometimes swims at speed, with its neck raised or lowered, and sometimes sinks down beneath the water. Could it indeed be a plesiosaur, as Sir Peter Scott suggested? Or does the scientific evidence rule this out?

For and against

Plesiosaurs were long-necked reptiles that lived in warm, inland seas during **prehistoric** times. They were thought to have died out some 70 million years ago, at about the same time as the dinosaurs. But there is no absolute proof that they do not still exist, and their shape certainly matches the photographs and descriptions of the Loch Ness Monster.

Scientists have used fossil remains to reconstruct the body of a plesiosaur. This model clearly shows how closely the plesiosaur matches the photographs and descriptions of the Loch Ness Monster.

So, could a small group of plesiosaurs have escaped **extinction** by taking shelter in Loch Ness, unknown to science? It seems unlikely. First, reptiles are cold-blooded animals. They rely on the weather to warm their bodies, which makes their bodies function properly. They would find it hard to live in the freezing cold water of Loch Ness. No reptile is known that could survive such cold conditions. Second, the **geological** history of the lake also seems to rule them out. For much of the time since the period of the dinosaurs, Loch Ness has been filled with solid ice as a result of a succession of **Ice Ages**. However, when the ice finally retreated about 11,000 years ago, it left the lake and a shallow passage to the sea: the Ness River. Could the plesiosaurs have swum up the river from the sea and entered the lake? It seems unlikely, though not impossible.

Other "lost" animals

Cryptozoology is the study of cryptids, or "unknown" animals. This means animals thought to be long extinct. One example is a fish called the coelacanth (say "seel-uh-kanth"). Thought to have died out 70 million years ago, a living coelacanth was caught in the Indian Ocean in 1938. Scientists were amazed. If the coelacanth still exists, what about other prehistoric animals? Could there be a plesiosaur still living in Loch Ness?

This is a coelacanth.

MAMMALS AND FISH

If science rules out the **plesiosaur**, what other type of
creature could the monster be? Other possible candidates
include mammals and fish.

A mammal?

Some scientists think that the Loch Ness Monster might be a
large mammal, such as a whale. Mammals are warm-blooded, so
they would be able to adapt to the cold conditions. But the largest
whales are **filter-feeders**, feeding on **plankton** in the water. The
small amount of plankton in Loch Ness means that the monster
could not be one of these (see below). Other mammals, such as
seals, need to leave the water to breed (mate), and there have
been no sightings or traces of young. If the monster does exist, it
must be part of a group to breed and continue the line. Mammals
also need to surface frequently to breathe, so there should have
been far more sightings of the creature if it is a mammal.

Finding food

If a large creature exists in Loch Ness, it probably eats
fish. However, it seems unlikely that the lake's fish supply
is large enough to support a large **predator**. Despite the
lake's great size, the water is poor in **nutrients** to start
the food chain. There is very little light for plant plankton
to grow, and, therefore, little for animal plankton to feed
on, which in turn would provide food for larger creatures
such as fish. As a result, there are very few fish for
such a large lake—or for a hungry monster.

A fish?

If there is a large creature in Loch Ness, it is more likely to be a large fish. Some people think that it could be a giant eel or a Baltic sturgeon, the largest types of fish found in freshwater. It is possible that the sturgeon enters the lake looking for a mate. When it does not find one, it swims out to sea again. Both types of fish can grow more than 10 feet (3 meters) long. However, none of the descriptions of sightings match any known fish closely. What scientists need is to examine a specimen or some actual remains of the creature, but nothing has been found so far.

Among the largest fish are basking sharks which, like whales, feed on plankton. They can reach more than 36 feet (11 meters) in length. They regularly appear in British waters in summer, when they swim inshore during their annual **migration**. In winter, they disappear again. One theory is that they move into deep water to **hibernate**. Could this deep water be Loch Ness?

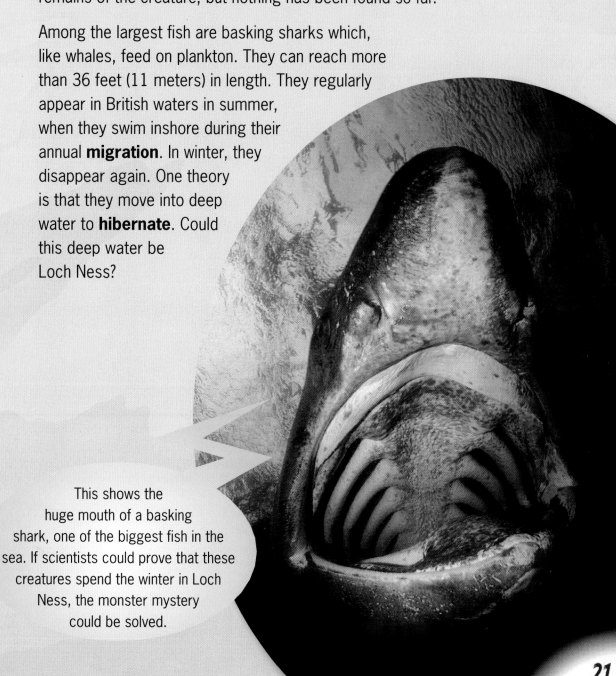

This shows the huge mouth of a basking shark, one of the biggest fish in the sea. If scientists could prove that these creatures spend the winter in Loch Ness, the monster mystery could be solved.

WAVES, WAKES, AND WATERSPOUTS

**People who do not believe that the lake is home
to a large, mysterious creature put down many of
the eyewitness sightings to odd waves and shadows
on the lake's surface, the wakes left by passing
boats, or weird weather phenomena. So, just
how misleading can these be?**

Waves and wakes

In rough weather, the wakes from passing boats are quickly
broken up by the wind and waves. Yet on calm days—on which
most monster sightings have been reported—the wakes last
longer and appear much bigger. From low down, the wake can
look like a rippling row of humps traveling across the water. Could
these explain the many accounts of a hump-backed monster?
Large waves breaking in the shallow water may also
be mistaken for a swimming body.

This wake was
photographed on Loch Ness in
August 1996. Mysteriously, it was a
clear day with no wind, and there were
no boats passing nearby.

Waterspouts

Waterspouts are spinning funnels of water that are sucked up by thunderclouds when they pass over water. The tallest ever seen was an amazing 1 mile (1.5 kilometers) high. At sea, terrified sailors often mistook them for monsters. Water devils are smaller versions of waterspouts. They spin across the water, whipping up spouts of water up to about 10 feet (3 meters) high. British tornado and whirlwind expert Dr. Terence Meaden believes that water devils may help to explain the mystery of the Loch Ness Monster. Their long, tapering, funnel shape could easily be mistaken for a monster's long, thin head and neck. Water devils also cause the surface of the water to bubble and froth. Could the rings of bubbles suggest a monster's humps?

Seeing things?

A mirage is an image of an object that is not really there. People have seen boats, buildings, and perhaps even monsters as a result of these **optical illusions**. Mirages are caused by changes in temperature in different layers of air lying over land or water. Light rays coming from existing objects can be bent up or down as they pass through the layers. Your brain is tricked into thinking that the distorted reflection looks like another object. For example, you may think you see a puddle of water on the road on a hot summer day. What you are actually seeing is a mirage of the sky. Could "Nessie" sightings be the result of mirages?

MONSTER FAKES

Many of the eyewitness sightings and photographs of the Loch Ness Monster have turned out to be hoaxes (fakes). Some are cases of mistaken identity, rather than deliberate fakes. But some have been carefully planned to deceive. Why do people do it? The obvious reasons are to gain fame or money. One person even went as far as to suggest that the monster was an elaborate hoax dreamed up by the Scottish Tourist Board to attract more visitors! Needless to say, this has been strongly denied.

The surgeon's photograph

One of the most famous photographs of the Loch Ness Monster appeared in April 1934. Nicknamed the "surgeon's photograph," it was taken by London surgeon Robert Kenneth Wilson. The photo clearly showed a long neck with a tiny head arched over the water. When the photograph was printed in the London newspaper the *Daily Mail*, it caused a sensation. But was it real? Many people thought so.

The most famous of all monster pictures is this so-called "surgeon's photograph." In 1994 the photograph was said to be a fake, but some experts have dismissed these claims. Is it a fake or is it genuine? The controversy continues.

In 1994 Loch Ness researcher Alisdair Boyd claimed that the photo was an elaborate fake. His investigation led to a man named Christian Spurling, who confessed to helping the surgeon plan the hoax in order to trick the newspapers. He said that the object in the photo was, in fact, a 12-inch (30-centimeter) plastic neck attached to a toy submarine, and not a monster at all. To answer his critics, Boyd set out to prove his theory. From the shape of the ripples around the neck, it was possible to calculate the angle at which the photo had been taken. Boyd lined up his camera and took some pictures of a 12-inch (30-centimeter) styrofoam neck he had placed in the water. The results were almost identical. Despite this, Boyd remains convinced that there is a monster in Loch Ness and claims to have seen it.

Monster footprints

In December 1933 there was great excitement at the discovery of a set of monster-sized footprints on the lakeshore. They were later found to have been created using an umbrella stand made from the stuffed back foot of a hippopotamus!

What's in a name?

Based on the **rhomboid**, or diamond, shape of the flipper in Rines's famous photograph, **naturalist** Sir Peter Scott suggested a scientific Latin name for the monster: Nessiteras rhombopteryx. Doubters discovered that you could rearrange the letters to read "Monster hoax by Sir Peter S"!

OTHER LAKE MONSTERS

Loch Ness is not the only lake where long-necked monsters are thought to lurk. Similar creatures have been sighted not only in other Scottish lakes, but in about 300 lakes all over the world, from North America to Southeast Asia. If hard proof were found for any of these, it would give a huge boost to the search for the monster in Loch Ness.

Lake Okanagan, Canada

Lake Okanagan in western Canada is thought to contain a monster called Ogopogo. Hundreds of sightings have been recorded. In July 1986 a man fishing on the lake reported, "It looked like a submarine surfacing, coming towards my boat. As it came up, we could see six humps out of the water, each one creating a **wake**." One woman reported almost running over it as she was out water-skiing. The local Okanakane Indians have many myths about a lake serpent. When crossing the lake by canoe, legend says, travelers always took a chicken or dog to sacrifice if the monster came too close.

This is a lakeside model of Ogopogo, the monster in Lake Okanagan, Canada. Sightings of this monster rival those of Nessie.

This photo, taken in 1977, added fuel to the rumor that there was a monster living in Lake Champlain.

Lake Champlain, Vermont

Stories of a monster in Lake Champlain, in Vermont, also go back hundreds of years. Nicknamed "Champ," the monster is often described as having a long, thin neck, with a dark body and several humps. The most convincing evidence for Champ's existence was a photograph taken in 1977 that showed a huge, long-necked creature. Despite close scientific analysis, the photo shows no sign of being faked in any way. Whether you see the monster or not, you can always try some "Champ's chips" (made according to a secret recipe) or listen to Champ 101.3 FM, the monster's own radio station, instead!

Lake Ikeda, Japan

The first photograph of Issie, the monster in Lake Ikeda, on the island of Honshu, Japan, was taken by vacationer Mr. Matsubara in 1978. Legend says that Issie was once a beautiful white horse living by the lake. One day, a Samurai warrior took her foal away. In despair, Issie jumped into the lake, occasionally surfacing, in the form of a dark, humped monster, to look for her foal.

WHAT DO YOU THINK?

So, can science really solve the mystery of the Loch Ness Monster? Despite the number of eyewitness accounts and photographs, scientists remain unconvinced. Eyewitnesses are often unreliable and photographs are relatively easy to fake. In the absence of concrete proof, such as an actual specimen or a skeleton, the monster seems fated to remain a myth.

Can the plesiosaur theory give us the answer?

Sounds convincing . . .

- Eyewitness reports usually describe a large, long-necked, hump-backed creature. A plesiosaur would match this description.

- Searches using sonar have picked up several large unidentified objects, which could be animals.

- There is no proof that plesiosaurs don't still exist.

- Other animals that were unknown or thought to have been extinct.

But what about . . . ?

- Plesiosaurs are thought to have died out 70 million years ago. Could such a large animal have remained undiscovered for so long?

- Plesiosaurs were reptiles. No known reptile could survive in the cold waters of Loch Ness.

- Since the time of the dinosaurs, Loch Ness was filled with ice for long periods.

The search for the Loch Ness Monster continues. This is a sonar research ship used by Project Urquhart to scan the lake in 1992. Several **expeditions** have gotten very close to finding something. But what that something is, nobody yet knows.

Those who claim to have seen the Loch Ness Monster do not have any doubts at all, whether science agrees or not. They believe that something large and alive is lurking in Loch Ness. After all, there are plenty of places for it to hide.

What about the other theories? Do you think any of them might be true? Look at the list of theories below and think about the pros and cons of each. Decide which you think are the most convincing.

- Eyewitness reports are **optical illusions** caused by shadows and boat **wakes** on the lake.

- What about the photographic evidence? Do any of the photos convince you?

- The monster is a modern animal, like a basking shark or a whale, that would not normally be found somewhere like Loch Ness

- Sonar hits suggest that there are large animals in the lake. Are these just **shoals** of fish or something bigger?

- All the eyewitness reports and photographs are fakes.

What are your conclusions? Are there theories you can dismiss without further investigation? Do you have any theories of your own? Try to keep an open mind. Remember that science is constantly evolving and new discoveries are being made all the time. Just because something can't be proved scientifically now, it doesn't mean this will always be the case.

GLOSSARY

animate something that is alive

cryptozoology study of prehistoric or ancient animals, thought to be extinct

expedition journey with a special goal

extinct plant or animal that has died out forever

filter-feeder animal, such as a whale or a large shark, that feeds on tiny plants and animals that it filters from the water

flotilla small fleet of boats or ships

geological related to geology, the scientific study of the rocks of Earth's crust

GPS (Global Positioning System) very accurate way of finding your position on land, sea, or in the air. Information is sent from satellites orbiting Earth to a computer on the ground. From the satellite signals, the computer finds your location.

hallucination when you think you see or hear something that is not really there

hibernate to go into a deep sleep or period of inactivity. Some animals hibernate during the cold winter months to save energy when food is scarce.

Ice Age time when snow and ice covered much of Earth. The last Ice Age finished about 12,000 years ago.

marine biologist scientist who studies life in the sea

migration long journey made by some fish, birds, and mammals between their feeding and breeding grounds

NASA (National Aeronautics and Space Administration) organization in the United States that controls the U.S. space program

naturalist scientist who studies the natural world

nutrients substances in the water that provide food and nourishment for living things

optical illusion picture that tricks the eye into thinking it shows something that it does not show

phenomenon remarkable or unexplained happening

plankton tiny plants and animals that drift on the surface of water and provide food for many other animals

plesiosaur long-necked prehistoric reptile

predator any animal that lives by feeding on other animals

prehistoric before recorded time

rhomboid diamond-shaped

sediment layer of mud, sand, and rock that lies on the bottom of a lake or river

shoal large group

sonar short for "sound navigation ranging." Sonar instruments use sound to map a lake or seafloor. Beeps of sound bounce off objects or underwater features and send back echoes. These are picked up by an on-ship computer and used to draw up a map.

superimposed placed on top of something else, such as something that is added to a photograph

wake track left on the surface of the water by a moving ship or boat

zoologist scientist who studies animals

Find Out More

You can find out more about Loch Ness Monster in books and on the Internet. Use a search engine such as www.yahooligans.com to search for information. A search for the words "Loch Ness Monster" will bring back lots of results, but it may be difficult to find the information you want. Try narrowing your search to look for some of the people and ideas mentioned in this book, such as "Robert Rines" or "Operation Deepscan."

More Books to Read

Townsend, John. *Out There? Mysterious Encounters*. Chicago: Raintree, 2004.

Yorke, Malcolm. *Beastly Tales: Yeti, Bigfoot, and the Loch Ness Monster*. New York: DK, 1998.

INDEX